' "You are my first passion, my divine friend, but you shall be my last." '

GIACOMO CASANOVA
Born 1725, Venice, Italy
Died 1798, Dux, Bohemia

In this episode taken from the twelve volumes of
Casanova's memoirs, written between 1789 and 1798, our
hero recounts his romantic involvement with two women.
He has already fallen in love with 'C.C.' and is ready to
marry her. Her parents are against the match, however,
and have shut her up in a convent on the Venetian
island of Murano. It is here that he catches the eye
of a nun known only as 'M.M.' . . .

CASANOVA IN PENGUIN CLASSICS
The Story of My Life

GIACOMO CASANOVA

The Nun of Murano

Translated by
Stephen Sartarelli and Sophie Hawkes

PENGUIN BOOKS

PENGUIN CLASSICS

UK | USA | Canada | Ireland | Australia
India | New Zealand | South Africa

Penguin Classics is part of the Penguin Random House group of companies
whose addresses can be found at global.penguinrandomhouse.com.

This selection first published in Penguin Classics in 2016
001

Set in 10/14.5 pt Baskerville 10 Pro
Typeset by Jouve (UK), Milton Keynes
Printed in Great Britain by Clays Ltd, St Ives plc

A CIP catalogue record for this book is available from the British Library

ISBN: 978-0-241-25224-6

www.greenpenguin.co.uk

Penguin Random House is committed to a
sustainable future for our business, our readers
and our planet. This book is made from Forest
Stewardship Council® certified paper.

1.

Nothing is more precious to the thinking man than life itself; yet in spite of this, the greatest voluptuary is he who best practices the difficult art of making it pass quickly. It is not that he wishes to make life briefer; rather, he wants amusement to make him unaware of its passing. And he is right, so long as he does not shirk his duties. Those who think they have no duties other than to indulge the senses are mistaken; it is possible that Horace, too, was mistaken when he told Julius Florus: *Nec metuam quid de me judicet heres. Quod non plura datis inveniet.** The happiest man is he who best understands the art of finding happiness without letting it encroach upon his duties; and the unhappiest is he who has chosen

* 'Nor will I fear the judgment of my heir when he does not receive more than I did.'

a way of life in which he finds himself with the sad obligation to plan every day, from morning till night.

Certain that M.M. would not go back on her word, I went to the convent's visiting room two hours before noon. The way I looked made her ask immediately if I was ill.

'No,' I replied, 'but I have been so anxious waiting for an all-consuming happiness that I may well look ill. I have lost my appetite, and the ability to sleep; if it is postponed, I cannot answer for my life.'

'Nothing has been postponed, dear friend; but what impatience! Let us be seated. Here is the key to the *casino* to which you will go. There will be people there, for we must be served; but no one will speak to you, and you need not speak to anyone either. You shall wear a mask. You will not go there until *half-past the night's first hour*, not before. You shall climb the stairway next to the front door, and at the top of the staircase, by the light of a lantern, you will see a green door, which you shall open to enter an apartment that you will find illuminated. You will find me in the second room, and if I am not there, wait for me. I shall only be a few minutes. You may take off your mask, warm yourself by the fire and read, for you will find books there. The door to the casino is at such and such a spot.'

Her description could not have been more exact, and I rejoiced that I could not lose my way. I kissed the hand that had given me the key, and the key as well, before putting it in my pocket. I asked her if I would see her in lay dress or in her present holy attire.

'I shall leave dressed as a nun, but in the casino I shall be in lay clothes. There I will also have everything I need to disguise myself.'

'I hope you will not be in lay dress this evening.'

'And why, if I may ask?'

'I so like you coiffed as you are.'

'Ah, I see. Since you imagine I have no hair, I must frighten you. Rest assured I have the finest wig possible.'

'My God! What are you saying? The mere mention of a wig overwhelms me. But no, have no fear; I shall find you charming in any case. Just be careful not to put it on in my presence. You seem mortified. I beg your pardon. I am sorry to have brought it up. Are you certain no one will see you leave the convent?'

'You can rest assured; when you circle round the island by gondola, you will see a little quay. It gives onto a room to which I have the key; the lay sister who serves me is trustworthy.'

'What about the gondola?'

'My lover vouches for the gondoliers.'

'Your lover is quite a man! He must be old.'

'Actually, no. I would be ashamed. I am certain he is under forty. He has everything, my dear, to make him worthy of love: beauty, wit, sweetness of character and fine manners.'

'And he pardons your caprices.'

'What are you calling caprices? He had his way with me a year ago. I knew no man before him, just as no one before you has inspired my fantasies. When I told him everything, he was a bit surprised; then he laughed and gently scolded me on the risk I would run were I to give myself to someone indiscreet. He would have liked at least for me to know who you were before going any further, but it was too late. I vouched for you, and he laughed to hear me vouch for someone I did not know.'

'When did you confide all this to him?'

'The day before yesterday, and I told him the whole truth. I showed him copies of my letters, and yours, which, when he read them, made him think you were

4

French, although you told me you are Venetian. He is curious to know who you are, no more. But since I myself am not curious, you have nothing to fear. I give you my word of honor that I shall never make the slightest attempt to find out.'

'Nor I to know who this man is, though he is as unusual as you are. When I think of the pain I have caused you, it drives me to despair.'

'Let's not speak of it; but take heart, for when I think about it, I realize that you could not have acted otherwise, unless you were a fool.'

As I took my leave she pledged her tenderness to me once again at the little window, where she remained until I left the visiting room.

That evening, at the appointed time, I found the casino without the slightest difficulty, opened the door and, following her instructions, found her dressed in the most elegant lay clothes. The chamber was illuminated by candles in holders placed before mirrored panels, and by three other candelabra on a table covered with books. M.M. seemed to me a completely different type of beauty from the one I saw in the convent's visiting room. Her hair was coiffed in a chignon accentuating its thickness, but my eyes merely glanced at it, for nothing would have been more foolish at that moment than to compliment her fine wig. Kneeling before her, bearing witness a hundred times to my gratitude by continuously kissing her beautiful hands, such would have been the preludes to the transports of a classical amorous combat, had M.M. not imagined it her first duty to defend herself. Such charming refusals! The strength of the two hands repelling the attacks of a respectful, tender lover, at once bold and insistent, interfered only slightly. The weapon with which she preferred to check my passion and restrain my fire was reason itself, meted out in words as passionate as they were energetic, and fortified at every turn with loving kisses that melted my soul. We spent two hours in this struggle, as sweet as it was difficult for us both. At the end of this battle, we congratulated each other, each claiming victory over the other; she for having defended herself from my attacks, me for having kept my impatience in check.

At four o'clock (I am still counting in Italian time), she told me she was famished and hoped I was too. She rang, and a well-dressed woman, neither young nor old and with an honest face, set a table for two.

Putting all that we might need on another table beside us, she served the meal. The dinner service was of Sèvres china. The meal was composed of eight courses, each of them brought out atop a silver box filled with hot water to keep it warm. The food was delicate and refined. I exclaimed that the cook must be French, and she confirmed this. We drank only Burgundy, and emptied a bottle of 'partridge eye' Champagne, and another of sparkling wine to lighten our spirits. She dressed the salad; her appetite was equal to my own. She did not ring again except to call for dessert and everything we needed to make punch. I had to admire the knowledge, poise and grace in everything she did. It was obvious she had a lover who had taught her. I found myself so curious to know who he was that I told her I was ready to tell her my name if she would only tell me that of the lucky man whose heart and soul she possessed. She answered that we should leave the task of satisfying our curiosity to time.

Among the charms on her watch she had a small rock crystal flask identical to the one I had on my watch chain. I showed it to her, praising the essence of rose that emanated from a small piece of saturated cotton inside it. She showed me hers, which was filled with the same essence in liquid form.

'I am surprised,' I told her, 'since it is very rare and costly.'

'And it cannot be bought.'

'Indeed the essence was created by the king of France; he made a pound of it that cost him ten thousand ecus.'

'Mine was a present someone gave to my lover, who gave it to me.'

'Mme. de Pompadour sent a little vial of it two years ago to Signor Mocenigo, the Venetian ambassador to Paris, through the A. de B., who is currently the French ambassador here.'

'Do you know him?'

'I met him that day and had the pleasure of dining with him. On the eve of his departure, on his way here, he came to say goodbye. He is a man favored by fortune, but likewise a man of merit and wit, and of distinguished birth, for he is the count of Lyons. His pretty face earned him the nickname of "Belle-Babet"; he has also published a small collection of verse that does him honor.'

Midnight had struck, and time became precious.

We left the table, and in front of the fire I grew insistent. I told her that even if she did not want to yield
to love, she could not refuse nature, which must be
urging her to lie down after so pleasant a supper.

'So you are sleepy?'

'Not at all, but one usually goes to bed at this hour.
Let me put you to bed and sit at your bedside, or else
allow me to retire.'

'If you leave me I shall be very unhappy.'

'Certainly not more than I would be in leaving
you; but what shall we do beside the fire until
daybreak?'

'We can both sleep in our clothes on the sofa you
see before you.'

'In our clothes? So be it. I can even let you sleep;
but will you forgive me if I cannot sleep? At your
side, and constricted by my clothing, how could I
hope to sleep?'

'Very well. In fact this sofa is a proper bed. You
shall see.'

She got up, pulled the sofa out at an angle, spread
out the pillows, sheets and covers, and I saw a proper
bed. She tucked my hair into a large handkerchief,
and gave me another so that I could do the same for

her, telling me she had no nightcap. Masking my distaste for her wig, I set about this task when I was greatly surprised by something utterly unexpected. Instead of a wig I found the finest head of hair. After a hearty laugh, she told me a nun had no other duty than to hide her hair from the profane; so saying, she threw herself down, fully extended, on the sofa. I quickly removed my coat, kicked my shoes from my feet, and fell more on top of her than beside her. She held me in her arms, and exercising an unnatural tyranny over herself, she hoped I would forgive her all the torments her resistance must be causing me.

With a trembling and timid hand, and watching her with eyes that begged for mercy, I untied the six wide ribbons that closed her dress in front, delighted that she did not stop me, and found myself the happy master of the most beautiful bosom. Time was running out. She was obliged to allow me to devour it after contemplating its charms; I raised my eyes to her face and there read an amorous sweetness that said to me, *be happy with this, and learn from me to suffer abstinence.* Driven by love and all-powerful nature, and in despair because she would not allow my hands to roam elsewhere, I did everything I could to guide one of hers to the place that might persuade her that I deserved her mercy; but with a strength greater than mine, she would not move her hands from my chest, where there was nothing of interest to be found. Nonetheless, this was where her mouth landed when her lips left mine.

Out of necessity or the fatigue of spending so many hours without being able to do anything more than continuously swallow our mingled saliva, I fell asleep in her arms, holding her close in mine. I awoke with a start when I heard bells chiming.

'What was that?'

'Let us quickly dress, my loving friend; I must return to the convent.'

'You get dressed. I want to enjoy the spectacle of seeing you masked again as a saint.'

'With pleasure. If you are not in a hurry, you may sleep here.'

Then she rang for the same woman, who must have been the great confidante of all her amorous secrets. After having her hair done, she removed her dress, placed her watches, rings and all secular ornaments in a secretary that she locked; she then put on the shoes of her order, then a corset in which she enclosed in a narrow prison the pretty children who alone had nurtured me with their sweet nectar, before finally donning her habit. When the confidante had gone out to summon the gondolier, she threw her arms around my neck and told me she would wait for me the day after next; at that time she would tell me what night she could come to my house in Venice. There, she said, we would satisfy each other in full. Then she left. Very happy with my fate, although full of unfulfilled desires, I blew out the candles, and slept soundly until noon.

I left the casino without seeing a soul and, well masked, went to see Laura, who gave me a letter from C.C., which went something like this:

Here, my dear husband, is a good example of my way of thinking. You will find me ever more worthy of being your wife. You must, in spite of my age, consider me capable of keeping a secret, and discreet enough not to find fault in your reserve. Assured of your heart's love, I am not jealous of your mind's fancies, which help you suffer our separation patiently.

I must tell you that yesterday, as I passed through a corridor above the convent's visiting room, I dropped a toothpick from my hand and had to pull a footstool away from the wall to look for it. As I bent down to pick it up, through an almost imperceptible crack where the floor meets the wall, I saw you yourself speaking to my dear friend Mother M.M. You cannot imagine either my surprise or my joy. These two sentiments immediately gave way to the fear of being seen and making some indiscreet soul curious. After quickly returning the footstool to its place, I left. Oh! my dear friend, I beg you to tell me everything. How could I love you and not be curious to hear the story behind this remarkable event? Tell me if she knows you, and how you met her. She is a dear friend of mine; I have spoken to you of her, but never thought it necessary to name her. It is she who taught me French, and who gave me books from her room that have educated me in an important area many women know little about. Without her, no one would have discovered the grave disease that almost killed me. She gave me linen and sheets; I owe her my honor. In all this she learned I had a lover, just as I know she has one too; but we have never been curious about our respective secrets. Mother M.M. is an incomparable woman. I am certain, dear friend, that you love her, and that she loves you too; and since I am not at all jealous, I think I deserve to know the whole story from you. But I pity you both, since anything you might manage to do can only, I think, irritate your passion. The whole convent believes you ill; I am dying to see you again. Come at least one time. Adieu.

This letter disturbed me, for although I could count on C.C., this crack could expose us to others. In addition, I now had to lie to my beloved, since love and honor prevented me from telling her the truth. In the reply I immediately sent her, I told her she must tell her friend at once that she had seen her through the crack talking to someone in a mask. As for my meeting with the nun, I told C.C. that having heard of her rare merit, I had had her called to the grating, introducing myself under an assumed name. Therefore she must refrain from mentioning me, for the nun had recognized me as the same person who went to hear Mass at her church. As for love, I assured her there was nothing between us, although I agreed that she was a charming woman.

On Ste. Catherine's day, C.C.'s name day, I went to Mass in the convent's church. As I was walking to the *traghetto* to take a gondola, I noticed I was being followed. But I needed to be certain of it. I saw the same man also take a gondola and follow me; this might have been a coincidence, but in order to make certain, I disembarked in Venice at the Palazzo Morosini del Giardino and saw the same man like-wise descend. Now I was certain. I left the palace, stopped in a narrow street near the Flanders post, saw the spy, and with knife in hand forced him into a dark corner with the point at his throat, insisting he tell me on whose command he was following me. He might have told me everything had someone not appeared on the street by chance. And so he escaped and I learned nothing. But seeing that it was only too easy for a curious person to find out who I was if he so desired, I decided henceforth to go to Murano only masked, or at night.

The next day, when M.M. was supposed to tell me how she would arrange to come sup with me, I went to the convent's visiting room very early. She appeared before me beaming with the happiness flooding her soul. The first thing she said was to compliment me on appearing at her church after three weeks of absence. She told me that the Abbess had been very pleased, because she was certain she knew who I was. I then told her of the spy, and of my resolution not to attend Mass in her church any more. She replied that it would be wise for me to come to Murano as little as possible. She then told me in detail of the crack in the old floorboards, and informed me it had already been sealed. She said she had been fore-warned by a boarder at the convent who was very attached to her, but did not name her.

After these small matters, I asked her if my happiness was to be postponed, and she said only by twenty-four hours, because a new lay sister had invited her to sup in her room.

'Such invitations,' she told me, 'are indeed rare, but when they do come you must honor them, or make an enemy of the person inviting you.'

'Can one not claim to be ill?'

'Yes, but then one must suffer visitors.'

'I see. If you refuse, they might suspect you've slipped out.'

'Not at all. They do not consider that a possibility.'

'Are you then the only one capable of this miracle?'

'Rest assured that I am the only one, and that gold is the all-powerful god that creates this miracle. So tell me where you would like to wait for me tomorrow two hours after sunset.'

'Can't I wait for you here in your casino?'

'No, for the person who will take me to Venice is my lover.'

'Your lover?'

'Himself.'

'How unusual. Then I shall wait for you in Piazza Santi Giovanni e Paolo behind the pedestal of the equestrian statue of Bartolomeo Colleoni of Bergamo.'

'I have never seen that statue, or that square, except in a print; but I shall be there. You've told me enough. Only very bad weather could prevent me from coming; but let's hope for clear skies. Adieu, then. We shall speak at length tomorrow evening, and if we sleep, we shall fall asleep contented.'

I had to move quickly, since I did not have a casino of my own. I hired a second rower and was in Piazza San Marco in less than a quarter of an hour. After spending five or six hours looking at a great many casini, I chose the most elegant, and therefore the most expensive. It had belonged to Lord Holderness, the English ambassador, who had sold it at a good price to a cook when he left. This man rented it to me until Easter for a hundred sequins paid in advance, on the condition that he himself would cook the dinners and suppers I might give.

The casino had five rooms, furnished in exquisite taste. Everything in it had been made for the pleasures of love, good food, and the joys of the senses. Meals were served through a blind window set into the wall, containing a revolving dumb-waiter which filled the space completely so that masters and servants could not see one another. This room was adorned with mirrors, chandeliers and a superb pierglass above a white marble fireplace decorated with small painted tiles of Chinese porcelain, whose interest lay in their depictions of amorous couples in their natural state, kindling the imagination with their voluptuous positions. Small armchairs matched the sofas to the left and right. Another room was octagonal, and adorned entirely with mirrors, including the floor and ceiling; all these facing mirrors reflected the same objects from countless different points of view. This room adjoined an alcove with two secret doors to a dressing room on one side, and on the other a boudoir with a bathtub and an English-style water-closet. All the wainscotting was embossed in ormolu or painted with flowers and arabesques.

After telling the cook to put sheets on the bed, candles in all the chandeliers and candelabra in each room, I ordered supper for two for the same evening, assuring him that for wine I wanted only Burgundy and Champagne, and no more than eight courses, leaving the choice up to him, regardless of expense. The dessert was his choice as well. Taking the key to the front door, I warned him that when I entered I did not want to see anyone. The supper was to be ready at the second hour after sunset and served when I rang. I noticed with pleasure that the clock in the alcove had an alarm, for in spite of my love I was beginning to surrender to the sway to sleep.

After giving these orders, I went off to a milliner's shop to buy slippers and a nightcap trimmed with a double ruffle of Alençon point. I put these in my pocket. Since I was to entertain the most beautiful sultana of the Lord of the Universe, I wanted to make certain the day before that everything would be in order. Having told her I had a casino, I must not appear at all unfamiliar with it.

The cook was surprised when I arrived alone at two hours after sunset. I immediately criticized him for not having illuminated the place, since I had told

him the time and he could not have had any doubt
about it.

'I shall not forget a second time.'

'Light the candles, then, and serve.'

'But you told me for two.'

'Serve for two. Remain present at my supper this
first time, so that I may tell you everything I find
good or bad.'

The supper arrived in the dumb-waiter in good
order, two dishes at a time; I commented on everything, but found everything, served on Saxon
porcelain, to be excellent: game, sturgeon, truffles,
oysters and perfect wines. I reproached him only for
having forgotten to put hard-boiled eggs, anchovies
and mixed oil and vinegar on a plate for the salad.
He looked up to heaven contritely, accusing himself
of a great mistake. I also told him that next time I
would like to have bitter oranges to flavor the punch,
and that I wanted rum, not arrack. After two hours
at table, I told him to bring me the list of expenses.
He brought it fifteen minutes later, and I was quite
content. After paying, I ordered him to bring me
coffee when I rang, and then retired to an excellent
bed in the alcove. The bed and the fine supper

rewarded me with the sweetest sleep possible. Otherwise the thought that I was to have my goddess beside me in this very bed the following night would not have let me fall asleep. Next morning as I left, I told my man I wanted all the fresh fruits he could find for dessert, and ices in particular. To keep the day from seeming too long, I gambled until evening and found my luck no different from my love. Everything went exactly as I wished. With all my heart I thanked the mighty genius of my beautiful nun for this.

I went to wait beside the statue of the hero Colleoni at the first hour after sunset. She told me to go there the second hour, but I wanted to have the sweet pleasure of waiting for her. The night was cold but magnificent, without the faintest wind.

At precisely two hours after sunset, I saw a gondola with two oarsmen arrive. A man in a mask emerged and after speaking to the gondolier at the prow, came toward the statue. Seeing a masked man, I became alarmed, dodged him, and was sorry not to have brought along my pistols. The masker walked around the statue, came up to me, and held out a peaceful hand, which calmed all my doubts. I recognized my angel dressed as a man. She laughed at my surprise, took my arm, and without a word we made our way to Piazza San Marco, which we crossed, and went to the casino, which was only about thirty paces from the Teatro San Moisè.

Everything was as I had arranged. We went upstairs and I quickly removed my mask, but M.M. amused herself by slowly exploring all the nooks and crannies of the delicious place into which she had been received, charmed to let me contemplate from every angle, and often straight on, all the graces of her person, and admire in her finery the lover who possessed her. She was surprised by the marvel of seeing herself from one hundred vantage points all around her and at the same time, even though she stood still. The multiple portraits that the mirrors offered her in the light of all the carefully placed candles were a novel spectacle that made her fall in love with herself. Seated on a stool, I attentively examined the elegance of her attire. She wore a coat of rose-colored cut velvet, trimmed with embroidered gold spangles, a matching hand-embroidered waistcoat that could not have been more sumptuous, black satin breeches, needlelace ruffles, buckles studded with brilliants, a priceless solitaire on her little finger, and on the other hand a ring with a surface of white taffeta covered with a convex crystal. Her *bautta* of black blond-lace was as handsome as could be in its fineness and design. She came and stood in front of me so that I could see her better. I looked through her pockets, and found a snuffbox, comfit box, flagon, a case of toothpicks, a pair of opera glasses, and handkerchiefs that filled the air with pleasant scents. I attentively examined the richness and workmanship of her two watches and her handsome signets hung as pendants from chains covered with small diamonds. When I looked in her side pockets, I found flat flintlock pistols with spring firing mechanisms, of the finest English workmanship.

'Everything I see,' I told her, 'is unworthy of you, but allows my astonished soul to pay homage to the adorable man who wants you to know that you are truly his mistress.'

'That is what he said when I asked him to bring me to Venice and leave me here. He added that he wanted me to amuse myself, so that I would be all the more convinced that the man I was to make happy deserved it.'

'That is incredible, my dear friend. A lover of this

stamp is rare indeed, for I could never deserve the happiness that already so bedazzles me.'

'Let me go unmask myself alone.'

Fifteen minutes later, she appeared before me, coiffed as a man but with her handsome hair unpowdered, the long curls grazing her chin on either side of her face. A black ribbon tied it behind her neck, letting it hang in a loose plait down to her knees. As a woman, M.M. resembled Henriette, and as a man a guardsman I once knew in Paris named *l'Etorière*; or even Antinoüs, of whom one still sees statues, had her French garb allowed me the illusion.

Overwhelmed by so many charms, I thought I was going to faint. I threw myself on the sofa to support my head.

'I have lost all faith,' I told her. 'You will never be mine. Even tonight some fateful mishap will tear you from my arms, perhaps some miracle wrought by your divine husband in jealousy of a mortal. I feel annihilated. In one quarter of an hour I may no longer exist.'

'Are you mad? I am yours this very instant, if you like. Although I've not eaten today, I am not the least bit hungry. Let us go to bed.'

She was cold, so we sat down before the fire. She told me she had not worn a waistcoat. I unfastened a diamond heart that closed her ruffle, and my hands sensed, before my eyes saw, that only her chemise shielded the cold from the two sources of life adorning her bosom. I grew ardent; but it took only a single kiss of hers to calm me, and two words: 'After supper.'

I rang and, seeing her alarm, showed her the dumb waiter.

'No one will see you,' I told her, 'you might tell your lover, who is perhaps unaware of this device.'

'He is not unaware of it; but he will admire your attention and note that you are not a novice in the art of pleasing, and that clearly I am not the only woman to enjoy the delights of this little house with you.'

'And he will be wrong. I have not dined or slept here with anyone else; and I abhor lies. You are not my first passion, my divine friend, but you shall be my last.'

'I shall be happy, my friend, if you are faithful. My lover is faithful and sweet; but he has always left my heart untouched.'

'His heart must be untouched as well, for were his

love of the same cast as mine, he would never allow
you an absence such as this. He could not tolerate it.'

'He loves me, as I love you. Do you believe I
love you?'

'I must believe it; but you would not tolerate—'

'Say no more; for I sense that so long as you do not
hide things from me, I shall forgive you everything.
The joy I feel in my soul right now comes more from
the certainty that I possess what is necessary to fulfill
your every desire, than from the idea that I am about
to spend a delicious night with you. It will be the first
such night of my life.'

'You have not spent such nights with your worthy
lover?'

'Yes. But they were animated only by friendship,
gratitude and kindness. Love is what truly counts.
In spite of this my lover is very much like you. He
has a lively wit, equal to your own, and a comely face
and figure as well, though he does not look at all like
you. I think he is even richer than you, although to
judge from this casino one might suspect the oppos-
ite. But do not imagine that I deemed you less
deserving than he because you have confessed yourself incapable of the heroism of allowing me an

absence. On the contrary, if you told me you would indulge one of my fantasies as he has, I would know that you did not love me as you do, for which I am very grateful.'

'Will he be curious about the details of this night?'

'He will think it pleases me to be asked how it went, and I shall tell him everything except a few small details that might humiliate him.'

After the supper, which she found both delicate and exquisite, as she did the ices and oysters, she made punch. After drinking a few glasses of it, in my amorous impatience I begged her to consider the fact that we had but seven hours ahead of us and would be doing ourselves a great injustice not to spend them in bed. Thus we went into the alcove, which was lighted by twelve blazing candles, and from there into the dressing room, where I presented her with the beautiful lace nightcap and requested that she comb her hair as a woman. Proclaiming the nightcap magnificent, she told me to go undress in the next room, promising to call me as soon as she was in bed.

This took but two minutes. I threw myself into her burning arms, passionate with love, and gave her the most ardent proof of this for seven hours straight, interrupted only by as many quarter hours animated by the tenderest exchanges. She taught me nothing new in matters of the act itself, but countless novelties in the way of sighs, ecstasies, transports and natural sentiments that arise only in such moments. Each discovery I made raised my soul to love, which in turn fortified me in the demonstration of my gratitude. She was astonished to find herself receptive to so much pleasure, for I showed her many things she had considered fictions. I did things to her that she did not feel she could ask me to do, and I taught her that the slightest constraint spoils the greatest pleasures. When the morning bells tolled, she raised her eyes to the Third Heaven like an idolatress thanking the Mother and Son for having so well rewarded the effort it had cost her to declare her passion to me.

We dressed in haste, and seeing me place the beautiful nightcap in her pocket, she assured me she would cherish it forever. After coffee, we walked at a brisk pace to Piazza Santi Giovanni e Paolo, where I left her, assuring her she would see me in two days' time. After watching her get in her gondola, I went home and, after ten hours of sleep, returned to my natural state.

2.

Two days later I went to the convent's visiting room after dinner. I sent for her, and she came at once and told me to go away, for she was awaiting her lover, but to come without fail the next day. I left. At the end of the bridge, I saw a poorly masked man emerge from a gondola, whose oarsman I recognized as being in the service of the ambassador of France. He was not in livery, and the gondola was as simple as all those belonging to Venetians. I turned my head and saw the mask go into the convent. I no longer had any doubts, and I returned to Venice delighted to have made this discovery and enchanted that my principal was the ambassador. I decided not to mention it to M.M.

When I saw her the next day, she told me her lover had come to take leave of her until Christmas time.

'He is going to Padua,' she told me, 'but everything

has been arranged for us to sup at his casino if we wish.'

'Why not go to Venice?'

'Not until he returns. He made me promise. He is a very prudent man.'

'Of course. When shall we next sup at the casino?'

'On Sunday, if you like.'

'Sunday it is; I shall go to the casino at dusk, and read while waiting for you. Did you tell your lover it was not unpleasant at my casino?'

'My dear friend, I told him everything; but one thing disturbed him a great deal. He wants me to beg you not to expose me to the danger of pregnancy.'

'Perish the thought. But do you not run the same risk with him?'

'Not at all.'

'Then we must be careful in the future. I think that nine days before Christmas, since we will not have masks I shall be obliged to come to your casino by water, since on foot I could easily be recognized as the same person who attends your church.'

'That is very prudent of you. I can show you the quay very easily. I hope you will likewise be able to come here during Lent, when God asks us to mortify

our senses. Isn't it droll that there is a time when the
Lord thinks it good for us to amuse ourselves, and
another in which we can only please Him by abstinence? What could an anniversary have to do with
divinity? I do not know how the action of the creature
can influence the creator, whom my reasoning can
only conceive of as independent. It seems to me that
had God made man capable of offending Him, man
would be right to do everything forbidden to him,
if only to help Him learn how to create. Can you
imagine God unhappy during Lent?'

'My divine love, you reason beautifully; but might
I ask where you learned to reason, and how you man-
aged to take such a step?'

'My lover gave me many books, and the light of
truth burned through the clouds of superstition weigh-
ing down upon my intellect. I assure you that when I
think about myself, my happiness at having found
someone to enlighten me is greater than my unhap-
piness at having taken the veil, since the greatest
pleasure is to live and die peacefully, which we cannot
hope to do if we believe what the priests tell us.'

'How true. But let me admire you, since the task
of enlightening a mind so prejudiced as yours must

have been at the time could not have been accomplished in only a few months.'

'I would have seen the light a lot less soon had I been less filled with misconceptions. What separated the true from the false in my mind was merely a veil; only reason itself could lift it, but I had been taught to disdain reason. Once I was shown that I must make the most of it, I put it to work at once, and the veil was lifted. The truth suddenly became clearly manifest, and all my silly notions disappeared. I need not worry that they will reappear, for I fortify myself against them daily. I can say that I did not begin to love God until I disabused myself of the idea religion had given me of Him.'

'Congratulations. You have been more fortunate than I. You have made more progress in one year than I have in ten.'

'So you did not begin by reading what Lord Bolimbroke has written? Five or six months ago I was reading Charron's *La Sagesse* and I don't know how our confessor found out. He had the audacity to tell me during confession that I should stop reading it. I responded that since it did not disturb my conscience, I could not obey him. He told me he would not absolve me, and I answered that I would take communion anyway. The priest went to Bishop Diedo to ask what he should do, and the bishop came to talk to me, insinuating that I should follow my confessor. I told him that my confessor's job was to absolve me, and that he had no right to give me unsolicited advice. I told him outright that it was his duty not to create a scandal in the convent, and that if he would not absolve me, I would take communion anyway. The bishop told him to leave me to my own conscience. But I was not satisfied. My lover obtained a papal brief allowing me to confess myself to whomever I pleased. All my sisters are jealous of this privilege; but I have used it only once, since it is not worth the trouble. I still confess to the same priest, who after hearing me out has no problem absolving me, since I tell him nothing of any importance.'

Thus did I come to recognize a charming freethinker in this woman; yet it could not have been otherwise, since she needed more to pacify her conscience than to satisfy her senses.

After assuring her she would find me at the casino, I returned to Venice. Sunday after dinner, I circled the island of Murano in a gondola with two oarsmen, as much to see where the casino's quay might be, as to find the small quay by which she left the convent. But I could not make out a thing. I did not find the casino's quay until the novena, and the convent's small quay until six months later, at great risk to my life.

About an hour after sunset I went to the temple of my love, and while awaiting my idol's arrival, I amused myself examining the books that made up the small library in the boudoir. They were few but well-chosen. It contained everything the wisest philosophers had written against religion, and all that the most voluptuous minds had penned on the unparalleled subject of love. These were seductive books whose incendiary style drives the reader to seek reality, the only possible means of quelling the fires he feels circulating in his veins. Besides these books, there was an *in folio* containing only erotic prints. Their great merit lay more in the beauty of their execution than the lewdness of the positions depicted. I recognized engravings for the *Portier des Chartreux* made in England, as well as others for Meursius or Aloysia Sigea Toletana, which were more beautiful than anything I had ever seen. Aside from these, the room was decorated with small paintings so well-executed that the figures seemed alive. An hour went by in no time.

When M.M. appeared dressed as a nun, I cried out. I told her, as I flung my arms around her neck, that she could not have come more fittingly attired to prevent the adolescent masturbation to which everything I had seen the previous hour would have driven me.

'But in your saintly dress you astonish me. Allow me to adore you on the spot, my angel.'

'I shall don my lay attire at once. I need but fifteen minutes. I do not like myself in these woolens.'

'Not at all. You shall receive my amorous homage in the clothing you wore when you first kindled it.'

She answered me with the most devout *fiat voluntas tua** as she dropped onto the large sofa, where I had maneuvered her despite her resistance. Afterwards, I helped her to undress and to put on a simple shift of Peking muslin, which was as elegant as could be. Next I became her lady-in-waiting as she arranged her hair in a nightcap.

After supper, before we went to bed, we resolved

* 'Thy will be done'

not to see each other until the first day of the novena when masks are not worn, since the theaters are closed for ten days. She then gave me the keys to the door giving onto the quay. A blue ribbon tied to the window above it would be the signal that would allow me to recognize it by day, so that I could go there later by night. But what delighted her no end was that I had gone to live in the casino and would not leave until her lover's return. In the ten days I stayed there I had her four times, and thus convinced her I lived for her alone. I amused myself by reading and by writing to C.C., although my tenderness for her had abated. The main thing that interested me in the letters she wrote me was what she said about her dear friend, the mother M.M. She told me I was wrong not to have cultivated her friendship, and I answered that I had not done so out of fear of being recognized. In this way I made her all the more obliged to keep my secret to herself alone.

It is not possible to love two women at the same time, nor is it possible to maintain a strong love by feeding it too much or not at all. What kept my passion for M.M. always at the same intensity was the fact that I could never have her without the greatest fear of losing her. I told her that inevitably, sooner or later, some nun would need to speak to her at a moment when she was neither in her room nor in the convent. She assured me that this could not happen, since nothing was more respected in the convent than a nun's freedom to shut herself in her room and make herself inaccessible even to the abbess. She had nothing to fear but the fateful event of a fire, when everything becomes so confused that it would be unnatural for a nun to remain calm and detached, and so they would inevitably notice her absence. She was pleased to have won over the lay sister, the gardener, and another nun whom she never wanted to name to me. Her lover's skill and money had guaranteed this arrangement, and he answered for the faithfulness of the cook and his wife, who were the casino's guardians. He also vouched for his gondoliers, although one of them must certainly be a spy of the State Inquisitors.

On Christmas Eve she told me her lover was about to arrive, and that on St. Stephen's day she was to go to the opera with him and sup with him at the casino on the third day of Christmas. After telling me she would expect me for supper on the last day of the year, she gave me a letter, requesting that I wait until I got home to read it.

An hour before daybreak, I packed my belongings and went to the Bragadin palace. I was impatient to read the letter she had given me, and immediately shut myself in my room. It said:

I was somewhat hurt, my love, when the day before yesterday, in regard to the secret I must keep from you concerning my lover, you said that although you are content to possess my heart, you leave me mistress of my mind. This division of heart and mind is a fallacious distinction, and even if you do not see it this way, you must agree that you do not love me completely, since it is impossible for me to exist without my mind, and for you to cherish my heart if my mind is not in accord with it. If your love can content itself with the contrary, it is not of the most delicate.

But since you could, one day, convince me that I haven't been as sincere with you as true love demands, I have decided to reveal a secret regarding my lover to you, although I know that he is convinced I shall never reveal it, since it would be a betrayal. You shall not, however, love me any the less for it. I find myself forced to choose between the two of you, and to betray one or the other; love has won out, but not blindly. You shall weigh the reasons that have tipped the scale in your favor.

When I could no longer resist the desire to know you more intimately, I could not satisfy myself without confiding in my lover. I never doubted he would comply with my wishes. He formed a very favorable opinion of your character when he read your first letter, in which you chose the convent's visiting room for our meeting, and he found you honorable when, after we became acquainted, you chose the casino in Murano over your own. But as soon as he learned this, he also asked me to allow him to be present at our first meeting, in a perfect hiding-place from which he would not only see what we did without being seen, but also hear everything we said. It is an utterly secret room. You did not find it during the ten days you spent in the casino; but I will show it to you on the last day of the year. You tell me if I could have refused him this pleasure. I agreed to it, and it seemed only natural to leave you in the dark. Now you know that my lover was present for everything we said and did during our first encounter. But please do not let this disturb you, my dearest. He liked you; not only for the way you acted, but for all the charming things you said to make me laugh. I became anxious when the conversation turned to the type of character my lover must have to tolerate such excessiveness; but luckily everything you said was flattering to him. This is the complete confession of my betrayal, which as a good lover you must forgive me all the more as it did you no harm. I can assure you that my lover is very curious indeed to know who you are. That night you were natural and very likable; had you known you were to have a witness, God knows how you might have acted. Had I told you about it, it is quite possible you would not have consented, and you might have been right.

But now I must risk everything to put my mind at ease, so that I may be exempt from reproach hereafter. You should know, my dearest, that on the last day of the year my lover will be at the casino, and that he will not leave until the following day. You will not see him, but he will see everything. Since you are not supposed to know this, you can imagine how natural you must appear, for if you do not, my lover will suspect I have betrayed him, since he is very intelligent. The thing you must keep foremost in mind is to be careful of what you say. He is virtuous in every area except the theological subject of faith, and in this you have free rein. You may speak of literature, travels, politics and tell as many anecdotes as you like, and be assured of his approval.

It is up to you to decide if you are willing to allow a man

to see you during the moments you surrender yourself to love's passions. This uncertainty now torments me. Yes or no? There is no middle ground. Do you understand how cruelly I am beset by doubt? Do you understand how difficult it was for me to decide what I should do? I shall not sleep tonight. I shall have no rest until I read your answer. If you reply that it is not possible for you to express passion in the presence of someone else, especially if he is a stranger, I shall then decide what course to take. Yet I hope that you will come all the same, and if you cannot play the role of lover like the first time, no unwanted consequences will ensue. For he will believe, and I shall let him believe, that your love has cooled.

This letter greatly surprised me; then after thinking it over, I laughed out loud. But it would not have made me laugh had I not known the sort of man who was to witness my amorous exploits. Certain that M.M. would be very uneasy until she received my response, I answered her at once, in the following terms:

My divine angel, I want you to receive my answer before noon. You shall dine without the slightest worry.

I shall pass the last night of the year with you. And I promise you that your lover, whose spectacle we shall be, will see and hear nothing to make him think for a moment that you told me his secret. Rest assured that I shall play my role to perfection. If it is a man's duty to be ever the slave to his reason, and if, so long as he depends on it, he should never undertake anything without it as his guide, I shall never understand how a man could be ashamed for a friend to see him give the greatest proof of his love to a beautiful woman. This is my position. You should know, however, that I think it would have been a mistake to tell me the first time. I would have categorically refused. I would have thought it a slight to my honor; I would have thought that in inviting me to supper you were merely obliging your lover, an unusual man, for whom this pre-dilection was perhaps pronounced, and I would have formed so unfavorable an impression of you that it might have cured me of my love, which at that moment was just beginning to bud. Such, my charming friend, is the human heart; but now the situation is different. All that you have told me of your worthy lover has allowed me to understand his character, and I think of him as my friend as well, and I love him. If no sense of shame prevents you from letting him see you show your love and tenderness to me, how could I, far from feeling ashamed, not feel proud? What man would blush at his own glory? I cannot blush, my dearest, for having won your heart, nor for allowing myself to be seen during moments in which I flatter myself that I shall not appear unworthy of this favor. I do, however, know from natural sentiment, to which reason cannot object, that most men find it distasteful to be seen during such moments. Those who cannot give good reasons for this repugnance must share some of the characteristics of a cat; they may indeed have good reasons, but simply do not feel obliged to account for them to anyone.

The first of such reasons might be that a third person looking on, and visible to them, would distract them, and any distraction might lessen the pleasure of coupling.

Another important reason, which could be considered legitimate, would be that the actors might think the means by which their pleasures were gained could arouse pity in the spectators who witnessed them. Such unhappy souls are right not to seek to rouse feelings of pity in an act that seems instead designed to make others jealous. But we know, my dear, that we shall certainly not rouse feelings of pity. Everything you have told me makes me certain that your friend's angelic spirit will, in seeing us, share our pleasures. But do you know what will happen? And I shall be sorry for this, since your lover can only be a man most worthy of love. As he watches us he will become enflamed, or he will

run away, or he will find himself obliged to come out of his
niche, go down on bended knee before me, and beg me to
surrender you to the violence of his desires, desperate to
quell the fire that our revels will have kindled in his soul.
If such a thing happens I shall laugh, and relinquish you
to him; but I shall leave, since I sense that I could not
remain a calm spectator to what another man might do to
you. So adieu, my angel; everything will be fine. I will seal
this letter at once, and take it to your casino in all haste.

I spent these six holidays with friends, at the
Ridotto, which during that period opened its doors
on St. Stephen's day. As I could not deal, since only
patricians in official dress were allowed to hold the
bank, I played from morning till night, and lost continuously. He who punts can only lose. But the loss
of my entire fortune of four or five thousand sequins
only intensified my love.

In 1774 the Great Council passed a law prohibiting
all games of chance, and closed what was called the
Ridotto. The Great Council was then astonished to
learn, upon tallying its votes, that it had passed a law
it should not have, since at least three quarters of the
voters did not want it passed. Yet in spite of this at

least three quarters of the ballots showed that they did. The voters looked at one another in astonishment. It was clearly a miracle of the glorious Evangelist St. Mark, who was invoked by Signor Flangini, First Corrector at the time and now Cardinal, and by the three State Inquisitors.

On the appointed day, at the usual hour, I arrived at the casino, where I found the beautiful M.M., dressed as a woman of society, standing with her back to the fireplace.

'My friend has not yet arrived,' she said, 'but I shall wink to you when he is inside.'

'Where is the place?'

'There. Notice the back of that sofa against the wall. All the raised flowers you see on it have pierced centers through which one can see from the room behind it. There is a bed there, a table, and everything a man might need to stay there for seven or eight hours, amusing himself by watching what goes on in here. You shall see it when you like.'

'Did he have it made himself?'

'Actually, no; he had no idea he would ever want to use it.'

'I realize this spectacle may give him great

pleasure; but when he finds he cannot have you at the moment nature makes him most desperately need you, what will he do?'

'That is his concern. In any case he is free to leave if he becomes bored, and he can sleep too. But if you are natural he will be amused.'

'I will be natural, but more polite.'

'No politeness, my dear, for that would hardly be natural. When have you seen two lovers trouble to be polite when given over to the passions of love?'

'You are right, my love; but I will be delicate.'

'Please do. You are always delicate. Your letter pleased me; your insights went to the heart of the matter.'

M.M. was wearing nothing in her hair, which was loosely arranged. A quilted sky-blue dress was her only attire. She wore small earrings studded with brilliants, and her neck was bare. A light silk gauze and silver thread shawl, donned hastily, exposed the full beauty of her bosom and highlighted the white-ness of her skin against the front of her dress. She was wearing slippers. Her shyly smiling, modest face seemed to say, 'Here is the woman you love.' What I found extraordinary, and what pleased me greatly, was the excess of rouge, applied in the manner of the court ladies at Versailles. The charm of these painted cheeks lies in the negligence with which the color is applied. It is not intended to appear natural, but rather to please the eyes, which see in it the signs of an intoxication that promises abandon and the transports of love. She told me she had put on rouge to please her lover, who liked it. I told her that judging from this taste, I was tempted to suspect he was French. As I said these words she winked at me: her lover had arrived. The play was about to begin.

'The more I look into your eyes, the more angry I am at your husband.'

'People say he is ugly.'

'They do. He also deserves to be cuckolded; and we shall work on this all night. I have been living a celibate life for a week, but I need to eat, for my stomach is empty except for a cup of chocolate and the whites of six fresh eggs I ate in a salad dressed with oil from Lucca and Four Thieves vinegar.'

'You must be ill.'

'Yes; but I shall be fine once I have distilled them one by one in your amorous soul.'

'I did not think you were in need of stimulants.'

'Who would need them with you? But I am understandably afraid, since if I *miss* you, I shall blow my brains out.'

'What do you mean by "miss"?'

'To miss, in the figurative sense, means to fall short of one's mark. Literally it means that when I try to shoot my enemy, the pistol does not go off. I miss.'

'Ah, I see. Indeed. Well, my dark-eyed love, that would indeed be a pity, but certainly not something over which you should blow your brains out.'

'What are you doing?'

'I am removing your cloak. Give me your muff too.'

'That will be difficult, for it has been nailed.'

'What do you mean nailed?'

'Put a hand inside. See for yourself.'

'How naughty! Did the egg whites give you this nail?'

'No my angel, only your charms.'

Then I picked her up; she put her arms around my shoulders to lighten her weight. Having let the muff drop, I seized her thighs and she braced herself on the nail; but after walking all around the room, and fearing the worst, I put her down on the carpet. Then I sat down with her in my lap, and with her beautiful hand she obliged me by finishing the task, culling the first egg-white in her palm.

'Only five to go,' she said, and after cleaning her pretty hand with a potpourri of aromatic herbs, she let me shower it with a hundred kisses. Now calm, I spent the next hour amusing her with funny stories; then we sat down to eat.

She ate for two, but I for four. The service was porcelain, but for dessert it was silver gilt, as were the two candelabra of four candles each. Seeing me admire their beauty, she told me they were a gift to her from her lover.

'Did he give you candle-snuffs as well?'

'No he did not.'

'Then I judge your lover to be a great lord, since great lords do not snuff.'

'The wicks of our candles do not need to be snuffed.'

'Tell me who taught you French, for you speak too well not to make me curious.'

'Old La Forêt, who died last year. I was his student for six years; he also taught me to write verses, although I have learned words from you that I have never heard him mention, *à gogo*, *frustratoire*, *dorloter*. Where did you learn these words?'

'In Parisian high society, from such people as Mme. de Boufflers, a woman of great insight who one day asked me why *con rond* was in the Italian alphabet. I laughed heartily, but did not know what to answer her.'

'I believe those are abbreviations used in former times.'

After making punch, we amused ourselves eating oysters, exchanging them once they were already in our mouths. She presented me with hers on her tongue just as I was thrusting mine into her mouth. There is no game more lascivious, or more sensuous, that two lovers can play; it is also comical, and its comicality spoils nothing, for laughter is only intended for the happy. And how delicious the sauce dressing the oyster I sucked from my beloved's mouth! It was her saliva. The power of love could not but grow as I chewed and swallowed.

She told me she was going to change her dress and come back coiffed in her nightcap. Not knowing what else to do, I amused myself by examining the contents of her secretary, which was open. I did not touch the letters, but opened a box and saw some condoms inside, which I put into my pocket. Then I hastily wrote the following lines, which I left in place of the stolen goods:

> *Children of friendship, ministers of grief,*
> *I am Love; tremble and respect the thief.*
> *And you, God's wife, shrink not from motherhood;*
> *If you conceive, He will claim fatherhood.*
> *But if to me your fruits you will deny,*
> *Speak up; I'll unman myself to comply.*

M.M. appeared in new attire, a dressing gown of Indian muslin embroidered with flowers of gold thread, and a nightcap worthy of a queen.

I threw myself at her feet, begging her to yield to my desires at once; but she ordered me to hold my fire until we were in bed.

'I do not want,' she told me laughing, 'to have to worry that your quintessence will fall on the rug. You shall see.'

Then she went to her secretary, and instead of the sheaths she found my six lines. After reading them, then reciting them out loud, she called me a thief, showering me with kisses in the hope of persuading me to return the loot. After reading my verses out loud again slowly, she pretended to think, then left under the pretext of looking for a better pen. When she returned, she wrote the following response:

> *When an angel f . . . s me I've no doubts*
> *That nature's author is my only spouse.*
> *But to keep His line above suspicion*
> *Love must return my sheaths without objection.*
> *Only as I'm subject to His holy will*
> *May my friend f . . . me fearless, as he will.*

I gave it back to her, feigning very natural shock; for it really was too much.

As midnight had struck and her little Gabriel lay pining for her, she arranged the sofa, telling me that since the alcove was too cold we would sleep there. The real reason was that in the alcove her lover would not have been able to see us.

While waiting I covered my hair in a Mazulipatan handkerchief, which, wrapped around my head four times, gave me the redoubtable look of an Asiatic despot in his harem. Having imperiously stripped my sultana to her natural state, and done the same to myself, I laid her down and subjugated her in accordance with the strictest rules, delighting in her swoons. With her buttocks raised by a pillow I had placed beneath her, and her knees bent away from the back of the sofa, she must have presented a most voluptuous sight to our hidden friend. After the revels, which lasted an hour, she removed the sheath and rejoiced to see my quintessence therein. Finding herself wet with her own distillations, we agreed that a brief ablution would restore us *in statu quo*. After this, we stood side by side in front of a tall mirror, each putting an arm behind the other's back. Admiring the beauty of our reflections, and becoming curious to play with them, we struggled in every direction, still standing. After our final bout she fell onto the Persian carpet that covered the floor. With eyes closed, head bent back, and stretched out on her back, with arms and legs spread as if she had just been cut down from a St. Andrew's cross, she would have seemed dead had the beating of her heart not been visible. The final bout had sapped her strength. I placed her in the upright tree, and in this position I lifted her up to devour her temple of love, which I could not reach otherwise, since I wished to place within her mouth's reach the weapon that had mortally wounded her without, however, taking her life.

Forced to seek a truce after this exploit, I placed

her upright again; but one moment later she challenged me to a return match. It was my turn to be the upright tree, and her turn to grab my hips and raise me up. Supporting herself on her two parted columns in this position, she was horrified to see her breasts splashed with my soul distilled in drops of blood.

'What is this?' she cried, letting me fall, and falling herself with me. Then the clock chimed.

I called her back to life by making her laugh.

'Have no fear, my angel,' I told her, 'the yolk of the last egg is often red.'

I washed her beautiful breasts myself, which no human blood had soiled before that moment. She was very afraid of having swallowed a few drops of it, but I easily persuaded her that even had this been the case, no harm would come of it. She dressed in her habit and left, after telling me to sleep there and to write her before returning to Venice, to tell her how I felt. She promised to do the same the next day. The caretaker would have her letter. I did as she said. She left only after half an hour, which she certainly spent with her lover.

I slept until evening, and upon awaking I wrote her that I felt fine. I went to Venice, where I kept my promise and went to the same painter who had painted my portrait for C.C. He needed only three sittings. I asked him to make it a little larger than the first, since M.M. wanted it mounted in a medallion and covered with a holy image to hide it from the world. She alone would possess the secret of uncovering it.

Casanova continued his relationship with M.M., spending time with her at balls, the theatre, the gaming table and even inside the convent. C.C., however, discovered the affair, took M.M.'s place at the pleasure-house and finally betrayed Casanova. Nevertheless, the three protagonists reconciled, after an exchange of letters. Casanova became friends with M.M.'s lover, the French ambassador to Venice, and a ménage à trois *developed, taking place between the ambassador's casino in Murano and Casanova's Venetian one (and becoming a* ménage à quatre *when C.C. joined in).*

Eventually, the ambassador was recalled to Paris and Casanova's passions for the two women cooled.

However, he soon found himself on the trail of new amorous adventures . . .